Declaring Our Independence

Kelly Rodgers

Consultants

Shelley Scudder
Gifted Education Teacher
Broward County Schools

Caryn Williams, M.S.Ed.
Madison County Schools
Huntsville, AL

Publishing Credits

Conni Medina, M.A.Ed., *Managing Editor*
Lee Aucoin, *Creative Director*
Torrey Maloof, *Editor*
Marissa Rodriguez, *Designer*
Stephanie Reid, *Photo Editor*
Rachelle Cracchiolo, M.S.Ed., *Publisher*

Image Credits: Cover, p. 1, 11, 18–19, 22 The Bridgeman Art Library; pp. 10–11, 13 Alamy; pp. 24–25 Emanuel Gottlieb Leutze, 1851; pp. 8–9 , 27 Getty Images; p. 24 Public Domain, 1976; pp. 26, 28, 28–29, 32, iStockphoto; p.12 The Library of Congress [LC-USZC4-2283]; p.15 Newscom; pp. 4, 7, 14, 20–21 North Wind Picture Archives; pp. 2–3, 6–7, 9, 16, 17, 18, 20, The Granger Collection; All other images from Shutterstock.

Teacher Created Materials
5301 Oceanus Drive
Huntington Beach, CA 92649-1030
http://www.tcmpub.com

ISBN 978-1-4333-6989-6

Table of Contents

Colonists work in the Virginia colony.

Strong Words

Americans have **rights**. We have freedom. We have the power to make decisions. This is because America is a free country. But it was not always free. Long ago, America was made up of 13 **colonies** (KOL-uh-neez). The people living in the colonies were called **colonists** (KOL-uh-nists). They were ruled by King George of Great Britain.

This is the Declaration of Independence.

IN CONGRESS, JULY 4, 1776.

The unanimous Declaration of the thirteen united States of America,

Declaration of Independence

A *declaration* is a spoken or written statement that can be heard or read by everyone. The word *independence* means freedom. So the Declaration of Independence was the American colonies telling the world they wanted to be free from Great Britain.

The colonists felt that the king was not treating them fairly. They wanted to form their own country. In 1776, leaders in the colonies sent a special **document** (DOK-yuh-muhnt) to the king. It said that America wanted to be free. This document is called the *Declaration of Independence* (in-di-PEN-duhns).

War!

The colonists had been **loyal** to Great Britain for many years. They had supported the king. But then, things started to change. The king made new laws for the colonists. He also made them pay higher taxes. This meant the colonists had to give more money to the king when they bought certain items.

Colonists read about higher taxes.

The colonists felt that they were being treated unfairly. They did not have the same rights as the people in Great Britain. They told the king how they felt, but he did not listen.

These colonists are marching against the Stamp Act.

Taxes

The colonists had to pay taxes on many goods. The Stamp Act made the colonists pay taxes on anything made of paper. They also had to pay taxes on tea.

By 1775, the colonists were angry. They were prepared to fight for their freedom. The first **battle** took place in Lexington. The colonists won. Then, they fought in Concord. The colonists won again! The American Revolution (REV-uh-LOO-shuhn) had begun. The colonists were at war with Great Britain.

These colonists are angry at the king for raising taxes.

The colonists fought hard. But some colonists did not know what they were fighting for. Some thought they were fighting for the king to give them rights. Others thought they were fighting to be free from Great Britain. The colonists looked to their leaders for help.

Colonists fight British soldiers at Lexington.

The Document

The leaders met in Philadelphia (fil-uh-DEL-fee-uh). After many meetings, they agreed that the colonies should declare their independence. They needed to be free from Great Britain. And they needed to let the world know about their plan.

This is Independence Hall in Philadelphia. This is where the leaders met.

A group of five men were chosen to write the Declaration of Independence. The men knew the document had to include three things. It had to describe what made a good **government** (GUHV-ern-muhnt). It had to explain what the king had done wrong. And it had to tell everyone that the colonies were free.

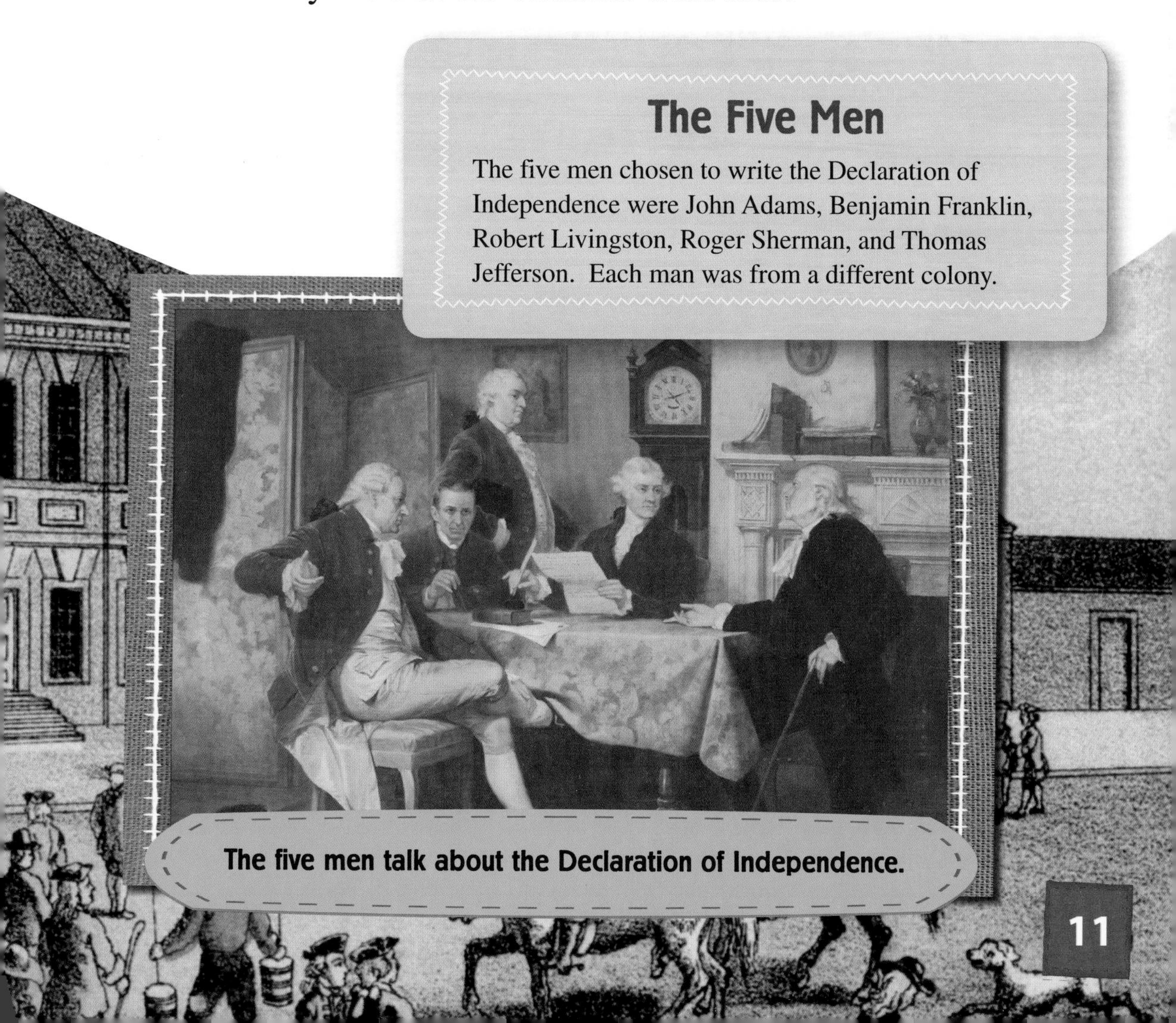

The Five Men

The five men chosen to write the Declaration of Independence were John Adams, Benjamin Franklin, Robert Livingston, Roger Sherman, and Thomas Jefferson. Each man was from a different colony.

The five men talk about the Declaration of Independence.

The group of men decided that Thomas Jefferson would write the document. He had written many other important papers. He was a good writer. The other men would review the document when Thomas was finished.

Thomas Jefferson

Thomas was a good choice. He was a smart man. He read many books. He knew a lot about history and **politics**. Thomas worked hard writing the document. He wanted to make his words strong. He wanted everyone to agree with him.

Thomas works on the Declaration of Independence.

The first thing Thomas wrote about was equal rights. In the document, he said that all people have rights. These rights cannot be taken away. It is the government's job to protect these rights. Everyone should be treated equally. Everyone should be free.

For All People

Thomas wrote in the document that "all men are created equal." He did not mention women. Long ago, most people did not think about women's rights. Today, we know that the Declaration of Independence speaks for all people.

Representatives of the UNITED STATES
[illegible]eral Congress assembled.
[illegible] of human events it becomes necessary for one people to
[illegible]ich have connected them with another, and to
[illegible]
[illegible] the earth the separate and equal station to
[illegible] of nature's god entitle them, a decent respect
[illegible] requires that they should declare the causes
[illegible] the separation.
[illegible] to be, self-evident; that all men are
[illegible]nt that they are endowed by their creator with
[illegible]enable rights; that among these are
[illegible]it of happiness; that to secure these rights, go-
[illegible] among men, deriving their just powers from
the consent of the governed; that whenever any form of government
becomes destructive of these ends, it is the right of the people to alter
or to abolish it, & to institute new government, laying it's foundation on
such principles & organising it's powers in such form, as to them shall
seem most likely to effect their safety & happiness. prudence indeed
will dictate that governments long established should not be changed for
light & transient causes: and accordingly all experience hath shewn that
mankind are more disposed to suffer while evils are sufferable, than to
right themselves by abolishing the forms to which they are accustomed. but
when a long train of abuses & usurpations [begun at a distinguished period,
&] pursuing invariably the same object, evinces a design to reduce
them under absolute Despotism, it is their right, it is their duty, to throw off such
government & to provide new guards for their future security. such has
been the patient sufferance of these colonies; & such is now the necessity
which constrains them to [expunge] alter their former systems of government.
the history of the present King of Great Britain is a history of [unremitting] repeated injuries and
usurpations, [among which, appears no solitary fact [illegible] to contra-
-dict the uniform tenor of the rest, [illegible] have] in direct object the
establishment of an absolute tyranny over these states. to prove this, let facts be
submitted to a candid world, [for the truth of which we pledge a faith
yet unsullied by falsehood]

Thomas wrote this copy of the Declaration of Independence.

The second thing Thomas wrote about was the king of Great Britain. He listed all the things the king had done wrong. He said that the king had taken away people's rights. He said that the king did not let them make their own decisions. Thomas said King George was a bad king.

King George

Thomas reads his document to Benjamin Franklin.

Finally, Thomas wrote about independence. He told the king that the colonies were free. The colonists were no longer **citizens** (SIT-uh-zuhns) of Great Britain. They were not loyal to the king.

This is the last page of the document Thomas wrote.

Thomas told the king that the colonies were forming their own country called the United States of America. They would have their own government. They would make their own laws. These were bold words to say. At that time, rulers, not citizens, ran countries.

Thomas shared his work with the other four men. They were all happy with the document. They thought Thomas did a good job.

Benjamin and John read Thomas's work.

On June 28, 1776, the five men shared the document with the other leaders. The leaders read the document carefully. They took time to think about Thomas's words. They liked what he had written. But they were still unsure about declaring their independence.

The five men present the document to the other leaders.

July 4, 1776

On July 2, the colonies voted. They voted yes! It was time for the colonies to tell the world they would keep fighting for their freedom. It was time for America to declare its independence.

One Last Vote

New York was the only colony that was not ready to vote on July 2. It voted "yes" a week later.

The leaders vote for independence.

On July 4, 1776, the Declaration of Independence was approved. The document was then taken to a print shop. Copies were made. The copies were read out loud to colonists. Soon, everyone knew about the Declaration of Independence.

The Declaration of Independence is read to the colonists.

Time to Sign

In August, leaders from all the colonies signed the Declaration of Independence. In total, 56 men signed the document. John Hancock was the first to sign. He signed his name in big letters. He joked that he wanted the king to read his name without having to put on his glasses.

American leaders sign the Declaration of Independence.

These leaders were brave to sign the document. They knew that if America lost the war with Great Britain, the king would not forgive them.

Old and Young

Benjamin Franklin was the oldest leader to sign the document. He was 70. The youngest leader to sign it was Edward Rutledge. He was 26.

General George Washington

The colonists knew they would have to win the war against the king's army to be free. They knew they would be punished if they lost. It was a good thing the colonists had a brave and smart **general** to lead their army. That general was George Washington.

George Washington

George was a leader from Virginia. He had fought in a war before. He was honest and made good decisions. He helped the army win many battles. In 1781, he made a trap for Great Britain's army in Yorktown. The trap worked. Two years later, the colonies won the war. America was free!

Off to Washington

A copy of the Declaration of Independence was sent to George Washington. He read it to his soldiers (SOHL-jerz) to inspire them.

George leads the American army.

The Declaration Today

The Declaration of Independence helped make America free. It helped start a new country. It gave the colonists a reason to fight. They fought hard for their freedom.

Happy Fourth of July!

We celebrate (SEL-uh-breyt) the Fourth of July each year. It is the nation's birthday. It is also called Independence Day. It is the day the United States was born.

These kids are celebrating Independence Day.

People are still moved by the words in the Declaration of Independence. It reminds them that America stands for freedom. It tells them that everyone needs to be treated fairly. It says that people should have equal rights. It is an important document in America's history.

These people are looking at the Declaration of Independence.

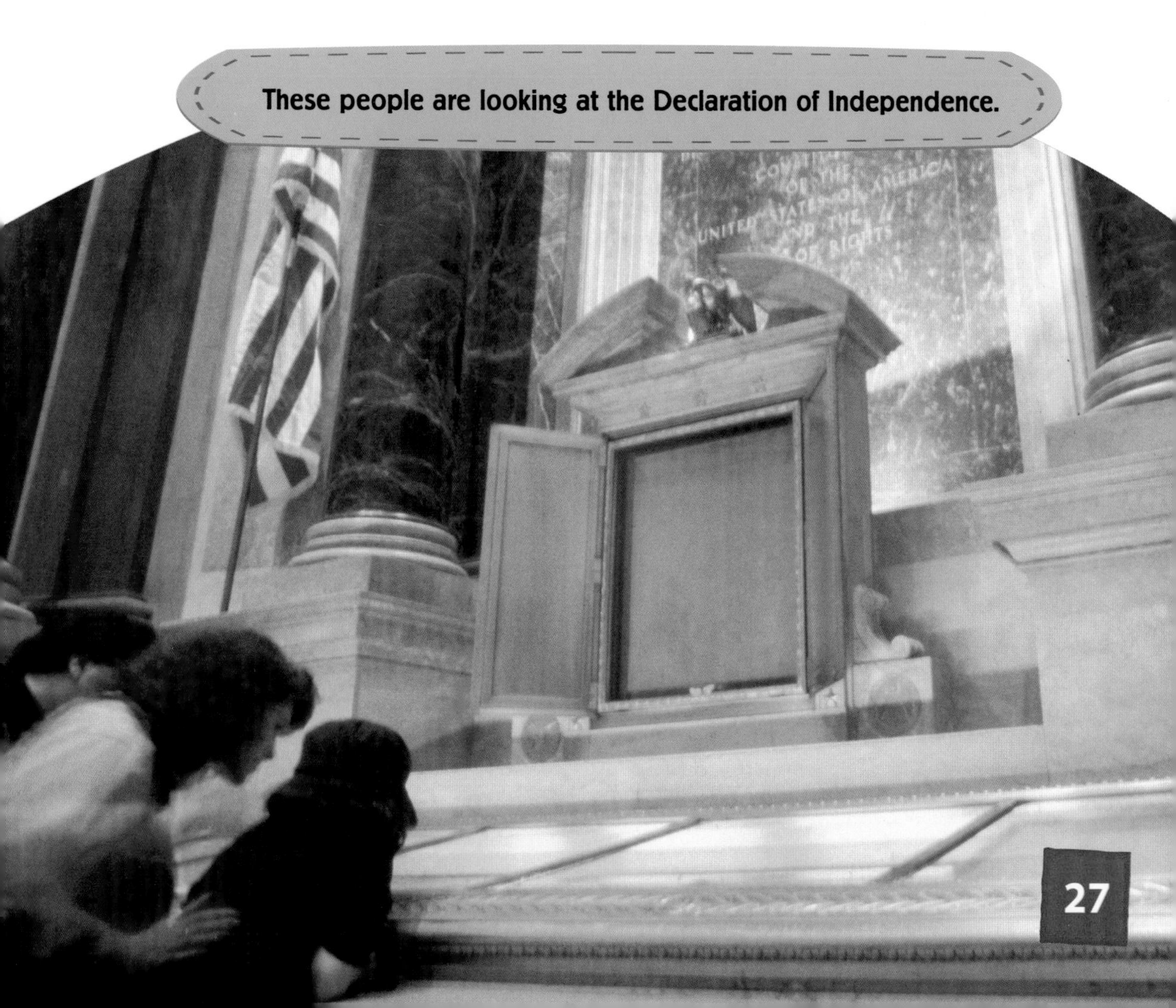

Sing It!

Learn the song "This Land Is Your Land." It tells about America. Sing it with your friends. Sing it to your family.

These kids sing the song "This Land Is Your Land".

This Land Is Your Land

This land is your land, this land is my land
From California to the New York Island;
From the redwood forest to the Gulf Stream waters
This land was made for you and me.

—Woody Guthrie

Glossary

battle—a fight between people or groups in which each side tries to win

citizens—members of a country or place

colonies—areas ruled by a country far away

colonists—people living in an area that is ruled by another country

document—an official paper that gives information about something

general—a military officer of very high rank

government—a group of leaders who make choices for a country

loyal—showing complete support for something or someone

politics—having to do with government

rights—things that people are allowed to have and do

Index

Your Turn!

Celebrate

The kids in this photo are celebrating the Fourth of July. This is also called Independence Day. Write a list of things you do to celebrate the Fourth of July.